16 WORLD DREAM TEAM!

4 TORRES!

38 HERE COMES THE WORLD CUP!

70 RECORD BREAKERS!

82 MEGA TRANSFERS!

10 THINGS WE LOVE ABOUT...
FERNANDO TORRES!

MATCH CAN'T GET ENOUGH OF THE LIVERPOOL STRIKER!

1

His 24 goals in 2007-08 is a record for a foreign player in their first Premier League season!

2

He hit the winning goal against Germany in the Euro 2008 Final with this cheeky chip!

YOU CAN JUST CALL ME 'LEGEND', MATCH!

3

His nickname, El Nino, is one of the coolest in footy! It means The Kid!

4

We've heard he's had three PlayStation rooms installed in his house!

5
Torres can rip the net with both feet and loves burning past defenders!

6
He's twice been named in the PFA Team Of The Year and won loads of individual awards!

7
Torres netted a hat-trick in just 11 minutes against New Zealand in June!

8
His Atletico Madrid captain's armband had 'You'll Never Walk Alone' written on it!

THERE'S PLENTY MORE WHERE THAT CAME FROM!

9
Liverpool's No.9 became the youngest ever Spain international to win 60 caps against Turkey last season!

10
El Nino scored his 50th goal for The Reds against Spurs on the final day of 2008-09!

FOOTY SHORTS!

MATCH BRINGS YOU A BIG ROUND-UP OF OUR FAVE FOOTY STORIES FROM 2009!

TOUGH

HOWARD'S JUMBO PADS!

> IT'S NOT FUNNY! MY SHINS ARE REALLY BIG!

> YOU'RE JUST JEALOUS, JAGS!

EVERTON: Phil Jagielka says team-mate Tim Howard wears the biggest shinpads he's ever seen! The USA keeper must have got them confused with cricket pads!

CHELSEA: Hollywood actor Will Ferrell reckons Chelsea's Frank Lampard is one of the hardest men that's ever lived! Ferrell said, "I love Frank Lampard! I think he's one of the toughest guys of all time!" How weird is that?

ROONEY'S VACUUM HELL!

> HELP COLEEN, IT'S GOT ME AGAIN!

MAN UNITED: Wayne Rooney reckons he's being haunted by a vacuum cleaner! Wazza's wife Coleen says he gets freaked out when the machine turns itself on without being plugged in!

PARKER'S BEACH BUDDY!

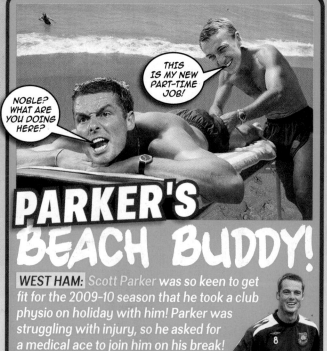

> THIS IS MY NEW PART-TIME JOB!

> NOBLE? WHAT ARE YOU DOING HERE?

WEST HAM: Scott Parker was so keen to get fit for the 2009-10 season that he took a club physio on holiday with him! Parker was struggling with injury, so he asked for a medical ace to join him on his break!

GUY LAMPS!

I'M GONNA PULL THE TEAM BUS TO OUR AWAY GAMES!

GOLDEN OLDIES!

TODAY'S BIGGEST STARS SWAP PLACES WITH FOOTY LEGENDS!

WHO'S PELE?

KAKA AS... PELE

I'LL BE DOING THIS NEXT SUMMER, ANYWAY!

JOHN TERRY AS... BOBBY MOORE

I'M ALREADY THE 'NEW MARADONA' MATCH!

LIONEL MESSI AS... DIEGO MARADONA

CAN ANYONE LEND ME A WIG?

WAYNE ROONEY AS... SIR BOBBY CHARLTON

ANDREY'S DREAM TEA PARTY!

I TAKE 15 SUGARS IN MY TEA, LOVE!

GET THIS GUY OUT OF MY HOUSE!

ARSENAL: Andrey Arshavin is desperate to meet the Queen! The Arsenal hero said, "I know the Queen has traditional tea parties, so I hope that one day I'll win the Premier League with Arsenal and get invited by her!"

BEST OF 2009...

CAUGHT ON CAMERA!

MATCH CHECKS OUT THE FUNNIEST FOOTY PICTURES OF THE YEAR!

Thierry Henry's so good, he can even run in the air!

THE GRASS JUST SLOWS ME DOWN, MATCH!

We always knew he was good in the air!

Worst dressed fans in the world?

I FOUND THIS HAT IN THE BIN!

Are all Wigan fans this crazy?

Is he gonna play on the 'wing'?

FOR MY NEXT TRICK, YOU'RE GONNA SEE A WICKED HAT-TRICK!

Gigi's been pumping iron!

WHO WANTS AN ARM WRESTLE! I'LL TAKE YOU ALL ON!

Has former Celtic hero Shunsuke Nakamura become a magician?

Juventus keeper Gigi Buffon is proud of his new muscles!

Mark Noble tries to convince Fabio Capello he should be the England goalkeeper!

Stick to playing in midfield, Nobes!

I'M MILES BETTER THAN DAVID JAMES, GAFFER!

DIZZEE RASCAL'S... HIP-HOP MAKEOVER!

Dizzee Rascal is the king of hip-hop style!
THIS WEEK: Stephen Ireland gets a new look!

BEFORE!

AFTER!

DUDE, THESE THREADS ARE TOTALLY FRESH!

YOU SHOULD BRING OUT AN R'N'B ALBUM!

WE SHOULD START UP OUR OWN FASHION LABEL!

Hates tomato ketchup!

WHAT AM I GONNA PUT ON MY BACON BUTTIES!

STARS' CARS!

DARREN BENT SUNDERLAND
Aston Martin DB9

PRICE: £119,850
TOP SPEED: 186MPH

NO-ONE TOLD ME IT RAINS IN ITALY!

Sammy's gonna cry!

Samuel Eto'o is already missing the Barcelona sun!

Fernando Torres can't believe the Liverpool canteen has run out of brown sauce!

IF PLAYERS WERE... GIRLS!

PURPLE IS SO NOT MY COLOUR!

CHELSEA'S DIDIER DROGBA WOULD BE... DIEDRE DROGBA

R U 2 BROT

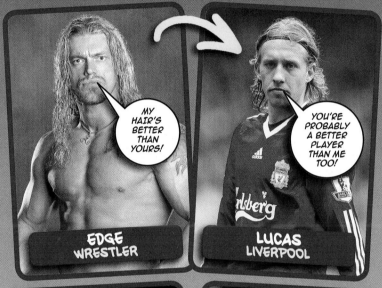

EDGE
WRESTLER

"MY HAIR'S BETTER THAN YOURS!"

LUCAS
LIVERPOOL

"YOU'RE PROBABLY A BETTER PLAYER THAN ME TOO!"

KEVIN KURANYI
SCHALKE

"I NEED TO GET ONE OF THOSE HATS!"

JACK SPARROW
PIRATE

HONEY MONSTER
CEREAL HERO

RICHARD DUNNE
REP. OF IRELAND

"HEY! I'M NOT THAT BIG, MATCH!"

DAVID MOYES
EVERTON MANAGER

"IT'S JUST LIKE LOOKING IN A MIRROR!"

MOE
THE SIMPSONS

FERNANDO VERDASCO
TENNIS PLAYER

"I'VE GOT A BETTER TAN THAN YOU!"

CRISTIANO RONALDO
REAL MADRID

"YOU WISH, PAL!"

BRAD FRIEDEL
ASTON VILLA

"GIMME A BREAK, MATCH!"

KURT ANGLE
WRESTLER

HERS?

FABIO CAPELLO
ENGLAND MANAGER

GOT ANY TIPS FOR ME, PAT?

POSTMAN PAT
POSTMAN

STOP PICKING HESKEY!

TOM JONES
ANCIENT POP STAR

WHAT SHALL WE SING, BROWNY?

PHIL BROWN
HULL MANAGER

I'M A BIG LADY GAGA FAN!

DOT COTTON
EASTENDERS

WE COULD BE SISTERS, NEV!

GARY NEVILLE
MAN. UNITED

I'M GONNA BE SICK!

FERNANDO TORRES
LIVERPOOL

THERE'S NO WAY I LOOK LIKE THAT MUPPET!

BRUNO
FILM STAR

THE TRUTH HURTS, TORRES!

DID YOU KNOW?

PICK THAT OUT, SHAY!

Cristiano Ronaldo only ever hit one hat-trick for Man. United. Ron's treble came in a 6-0 win against Newcastle in 2008!

WE SUCK, LADS!

13

THAT'S HOW MANY PREM MATCHES HULL WENT WITHOUT A HOME WIN BETWEEN DECEMBER 2008 AND AUGUST 2009!

CELEB FANS!

MATCH has heard that Conservative party leader David Cameron is a massive Aston Villa fan!

WHEN I RUN THE COUNTRY I'M GONNA CLOSE DOWN ALL OUR RIVALS!

THE NEXT BIG THING!

NEXT BIG

JOHN BOSTOCK
TOTTENHAM

TOTTENHAM'S ACE MIDFIELDER IS ONE OF THE HOTTEST TALENTS IN WORLD FOOTY!

JUST CALL ME BOZZIE!

FAVE POSITION!

BOZZIE SAYS: "I think the No.10 role, attacking midfield, is my best position, because I'm surprisingly quick and I've got a good touch. I can pick out a pass and I've got an eye for a goal!"

LIGHTNING SPEED!

BOZZIE SAYS: "My power and pace have both improved a lot. The whole Spurs squad did a speed test last season and Aaron Lennon came first, but I was second. I don't know how I did it!"

CAREER HIGHLIGHT!

BOZZIE SAYS: "It's got to be playing at Wembley in a friendly against Barcelona last summer. They didn't have all of their best players on the pitch, but they were still great!"

BEST GOAL!

BOZZIE SAYS: "My best goal was against Charlton last season. The ball came to me about 40 yards out and I thought, 'It's almost half-time, I'm just going to bang it!' I took two touches and just hit it. I was really happy when it went in!"

TOP TARGETS!

BOZZIE SAYS: "I want to have won the World Cup and the Champions League by the time I retire. A big thing for me is also to be named 'The World's Best Player!' But the most important thing is to know I've fulfilled my potential. That's really important to me!"

FAB FACT!
John beat 200 other players to win a place at the Crystal Palace academy when he was just six years old!

FAB FACT!
John won the South London Cup with his school team when he was in year eight, and hit 11 goals in one of the games!

FAB FACT!
Bostock made his league debut for Crystal Palace in 2007 when he was just 15 years and 287 days old!

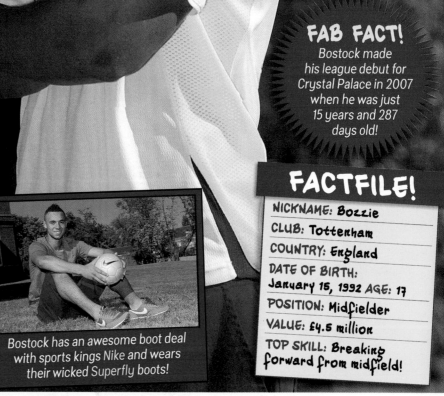

Bostock has an awesome boot deal with sports kings Nike and wears their wicked Superfly boots!

FACTFILE!

NICKNAME: Bozzie

CLUB: Tottenham

COUNTRY: England

DATE OF BIRTH: January 15, 1992 AGE: 17

POSITION: Midfielder

VALUE: £4.5 million

TOP SKILL: Breaking forward from midfield!

TOTTENHAM HOTSPUR

Arsenal

HEROES

2009

andrey arshavin

factfile!

age: 28

club: Arsenal

position: Forward

value: £30 million

country: Russia

footy fact! The classy Russia playmaker became Arsenal's record signing when they bought him from Zenit for £15 million in 2009!

REDS ST

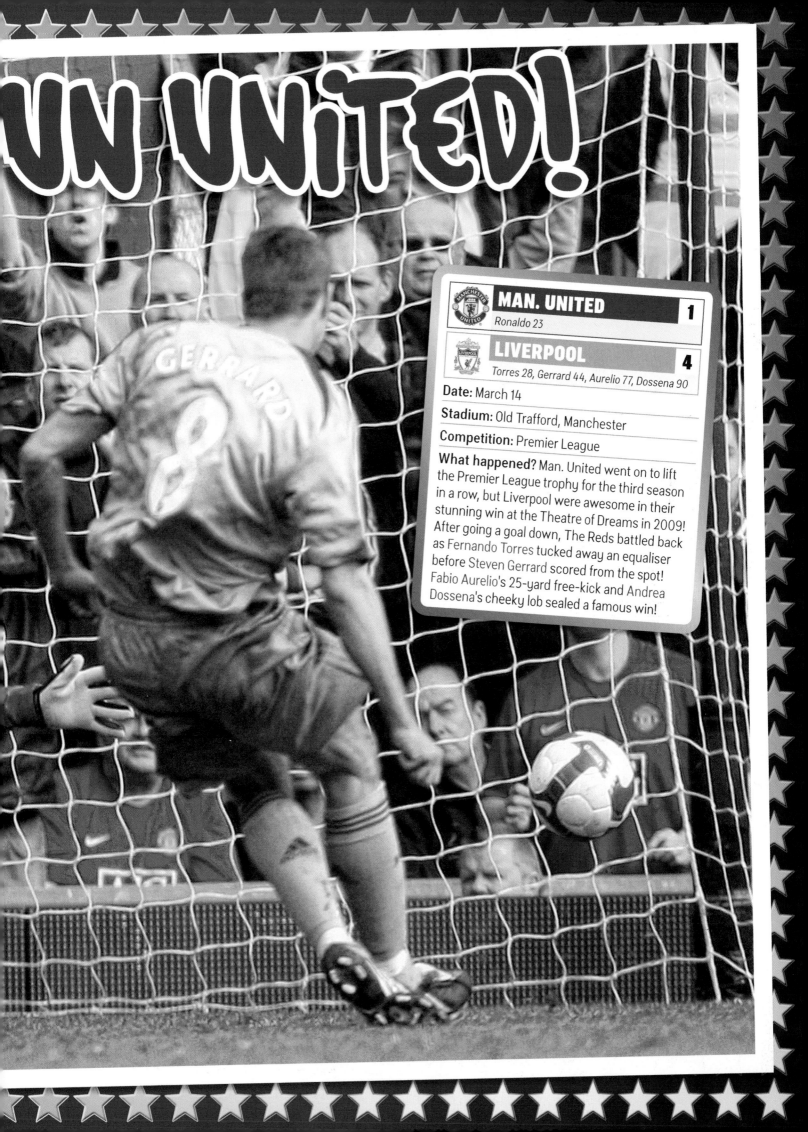

UN UNITED!

MAN. UNITED	1
Ronaldo 23	

LIVERPOOL	4
Torres 28, Gerrard 44, Aurelio 77, Dossena 90	

Date: March 14

Stadium: Old Trafford, Manchester

Competition: Premier League

What happened? Man. United went on to lift the Premier League trophy for the third season in a row, but Liverpool were awesome in their stunning win at the Theatre of Dreams in 2009! After going a goal down, The Reds battled back as Fernando Torres tucked away an equaliser before Steven Gerrard scored from the spot! Fabio Aurelio's 25-yard free-kick and Andrea Dossena's cheeky lob sealed a famous win!

WORLD DREAM TEAM!

MATCH HAS JETTED AROUND THE PLANET TO WATCH THE WORLD'S BEST PLAYERS IN ACTION! CHECK OUT OUR MASSIVE SCOUTING REPORT, THEN PICK YOUR DREAM XI!

WORLD DREAM TEAM!
goalkeepers!

pepe reina
Club: Liverpool ★ **Age:** 27
Country: Spain
Value: £15 million

Liverpool boss Rafa Benitez reckons his Spanish shot-stopper is the best on the planet! Pepe's won the Prem clean sheet award for the last three seasons and has kept over 100 shut-outs for The Reds!

edwin van der sar
Club: Man. United ★ **Age:** 38
Country: Holland
Value: £5 million

VDS is getting on a bit, but he's still one of the best keepers around! He's won 130 caps for Holland, lifted the Champo League trophy twice and went 1,311 minutes without conceding a goal in 2008-09!

iker casillas
Club: Real Madrid ★ **Age:** 28
Country: Spain
Value: £20 million

Spain's quality captain has won nearly every trophy in the game! Real's No.1 has bagged La Liga, Champions League and Euro 2008 glory – can he guide Spain to the World Cup final in 2010?

gianluigi buffon
Club: Juventus ★ **Age:** 31
Country: Italy
Value: £15 million

Footy's most expensive keeper has been playing for Juve since moving from Parma in 2001! The 2006 World Cup winner cost Juve a wallet-busting £32.6 million, and has been at the top of his game ever since!

petr cech
Club: Chelsea ★ **Age:** 27
Country: Czech Republic
Value: £16 million

Cech's been making world-class saves ever since arriving from Rennes in 2004! His awesome stops have helped Chelsea win two Prem titles, two FA Cups and two League Cups over the last five years!

WORLD DREAM TEAM!
centre-backs!

bruno alves

Club: Porto ★ **Age:** 27
Country: Portugal
Value: £10 million

Portugal's Player Of The Year couldn't stop crunching into opponents as Porto won their fourth straight title in 2008-09! The rock-solid centre-back is big, strong and almost unbeatable in the air!

john terry

Club: Chelsea ★ **Age:** 28
Country: England
Value: £30 million

Man. City were ready to pay Chelsea around £50 million to sign JT last summer – and it's not hard to see why! The wicked England skipper is a top defender who drives his team forward from the back!

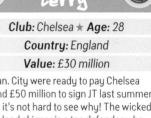

gerard pique

Club: Barcelona ★ **Age:** 22
Country: Spain
Value: £12 million

Man. United boss Sir Alex Ferguson must be gutted he let Pique return to Barcelona! The former Man. United defender had a quality season as Barça stormed to the treble in 2008-09!

ricardo carvalho

Club: Chelsea ★ **Age:** 31
Country: Portugal
Value: £10 million

Chelsea are gonna be a tough team to beat this season with Carvalho and Terry at the back! After losing his place to Alex, the rock-hard Portugal international has won his spot back under Carlo Ancelotti!

rio ferdinand

Club: Man. United ★ **Age:** 30
Country: England
Value: £25 million

Rio has rocked Old Trafford since he joined for a massive £30 million from Leeds in 2002! The United centre-back's passing, pace and tackling have led The Red Devils to three straight Prem titles!

jamie carragher

Club: Liverpool ★ **Age:** 31
Country: England
Value: £14 million

Carra hardly ever scores for Liverpool, but he's a master at stopping strikers at the other end of the pitch! The Anfield legend never seems to have a bad game and loves popping up with last-ditch tackles!

carles puyol

Club: Barcelona ★ **Age:** 31
Country: Spain
Value: £15 million

Puyol's got one of the girliest haircuts in footy, but that doesn't stop him being one of the hardest defenders around! He's won La Liga, Champions League and European Championship titles!

raul albiol

Club: Real Madrid ★ **Age:** 24
Country: Spain
Value: £12 million

Real's new £12 million defender can also play in midfield, but it's the back four where he's at his best! He can play at right-back or in the centre, and should become a big star at the Bernabeu!

giorgio chiellini

Club: Juventus ★ **Age:** 25
Country: Italy
Value: £10 million

Chiellini has played over 100 games for Juve since moving to Turin in 2005! After finishing runner-up in Serie A last season, Arsene Wenger was linked with a bid to bring the Italy hero to The Emirates!

nemanja vidic

Club: Man. United ★ **Age:** 27
Country: Serbia
Value: £30 million

The Serbia international's been a rock at the back for The Red Devils and was on the shortlist for the PFA Player Of The Year award in 2008-09! The giant defender loves smashing strikers around!

WORLD DREAM TEAM!
full-backs!

  sergio ramos

Club: Real Madrid ★ **Age:** 23
Country: Spain
Value: £25 million

Even the fastest forwards in the world can't get past the awesome right-back! Real splashed out loads of money on quality new players last summer, but there's no way they'll replace Ramos!

bacary sagna

Club: Arsenal ★ **Age:** 26
Country: France
Value: £20 million

The Arsenal right-back has become one of the best full-backs in the business since moving to England in 2007! He's got pace to burn and loves flying down the wing to whip in dangerous crosses!

dani alves

Club: Barcelona ★ **Age:** 26
Country: Brazil
Value: £25 million

The former Sevilla superstar has only played one full season at Barcelona, but he's already a Nou Camp legend! He gets forward so much that it seems like Barça are playing with two right wingers!

 maicon

Club: Inter Milan ★ **Age:** 28
Country: Brazil
Value: £25 million

Look out for Maicon at the World Cup, because the Brazil superstar is one of the best full-backs on the planet! The flying Inter right-back loves running with the ball and scores some world-class goals!

  miguel

Club: Valencia ★ **Age:** 29
Country: Portugal
Value: £10 million

Miguel has been a rock in Valencia's defence since he joined from Benfica in 2005! La Liga strikers hate facing the Portugal hero, because he always flies in with bone-crunching tackles!

philipp lahm

Club: Bayern Munich ★ **Age:** 25
Country: Germany
Value: £15 million

Wingers hate it when Bayern's full-back takes them on, because he's mega skilful with both feet! Lahm's not very tall, but he makes up for it with his mega energy and deadly crossing!

patrice evra

Club: Man. United ★ **Age:** 28
Country: France
Value: £20 million

The France left-back has been one of the first names on Sir Alex Ferguson's teamsheet since arriving from Monaco in 2006! The lightning-quick defender causes tons of trouble down the left wing!

javier zanetti

Club: Inter Milan ★ **Age:** 36
Country: Argentina
Value: £4 million

It won't be long before the San Siro legend hangs up his boots, but Zanetti's still a class act for Jose Mourinho's side! Argentina's most-capped player has starred in nearly 500 games for Inter!

gael clichy

Club: Arsenal ★ **Age:** 24
Country: France
Value: £24 million

Arsene Wenger paid Cannes a bargain £250,000 for the awesome left-back! Clichy has made the left-back spot his own since Ashley Cole moved to Chelsea – his pace and passing are world-class!

ashley cole

Club: Chelsea ★ **Age:** 28
Country: England
Value: £30 million

Cole must have rocket boosters in his boots, because he loves burning up and down the left wing! The England star is awesome at ripping down the touchline and curling in crosses for the strikers!

WORLD DREAM TEAM!
central midfielders!

andrea pirlo

Club: AC Milan ★ **Age:** 30
Country: Italy
Value: £18 million

The Serie A superstar has been creating chances and scoring wonder free-kicks from midfield for ages! Pirlo is a master at picking up the ball in front of his back four and launching wicked counter-attacks!

steven gerrard

Club: Liverpool ★ **Age:** 29
Country: England
Value: £40 million

Liverpool's captain is one of the greatest players to ever appear in the Prem! He's bagged over 100 goals for The Reds and always seems to come up with magic moments when his team needs him!

esteban cambiasso

Club: Inter Milan ★ **Age:** 29
Country: Argentina
Value: £22 million

Cambiasso is awesome at breaking up opposition attacks and getting the ball forward to his strikers! He never stops snapping at opponents' heels and has been a key player for Inter since 2004!

andres iniesta

Club: Barcelona ★ **Age:** 25
Country: Spain
Value: £40 million

When a player like Wayne Rooney says Iniesta's the best in the world, you've gotta take notice! His passing ruled La Liga in 2008-09 and he tore Man. United apart in the Champions League final!

frank lampard

Club: Chelsea ★ **Age:** 31
Country: England
Value: £30 million

Lamps is one of the best all-round midfielders in the world! Whether it's hitting long-range rockets or tucking the ball home from the spot, he always seems to be in the thick of the action!

cesc fabregas

Club: Arsenal ★ **Age:** 22
Country: Spain
Value: £35 million

Arsenal's young captain is one of the Prem's biggest names! Cesc's passing and vision are awesome, and he got his season off to a flying start with a brace against Everton in a 6-1 win at Goodison!

kaka

Club: Real Madrid ★ **Age:** 27
Country: Brazil
Value: £60 million

After all the hype around Ronaldo's move to Real last summer, it's easy to forget they also splashed out £56 million on Kaka! The Brazil playmaker rips teams to shreds with his killer through-balls!

michael essien

Club: Chelsea ★ **Age:** 26
Country: Ghana
Value: £30 million

Chelsea missed their midfield rock after he was sidelined with a knee injury for most of 2008-09, but now Essien's back! The Ghana legend runs games from the middle of the pitch with his mega power!

diego

Club: Juventus ★ **Age:** 24
Country: Brazil
Value: £20 million

Anyone who saw Diego's amazing brace against Roma in just his second game for Juventus knows exactly how good he is! The silky playmaker loves picking up the ball in midfield and driving at defenders!

xavi

Club: Barcelona ★ **Age:** 29
Country: Spain
Value: £25 million

Barça's classy central midfielder has played for the Nou Camp side his entire career! Xavi hardly ever gives the ball away and set up an amazing 20 goals as his side won the La Liga title in 2008-09!

WORLD DREAM TEAM!
wingers!

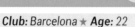

lionel messi

Club: Barcelona ★ **Age:** 22	
Country: Argentina	
Value: £100 million	

MATCH reckons Leo is the hottest player on the planet right now! The Argentina trick machine seems to win games all by himself and was Barça's star man in their 2008-09 treble-winning season!

andrey arshavin

Club: Arsenal ★ **Age:** 28	
Country: Russia	
Value: £30 million	

Russia's captain has taken the Prem by storm since joining from Zenit in January 2009! Arshavin knows when to pick out a killer pass and his shooting is unreal – he scored six goals in 12 games in 2008-09!

ashley young

Club: Aston Villa ★ **Age:** 24	
Country: England	
Value: £20 million	

Villa's rapid winger could become one of the Prem's best ever players! Young's devastating speed and quick feet leave full-backs standing still, while his curling crosses give goalkeepers nightmares!

yuri zhirkov

Club: Chelsea ★ **Age:** 26	
Country: Russia	
Value: £18 million	

The most expensive Russian player ever looks set to become a Stamford Bridge superstar! Chelsea's left-side is gonna be totally unstoppable with Zhirkov and Ashley Cole bombing down the wing!

ronaldinho

Club: AC Milan ★ **Age:** 29	
Country: Brazil	
Value: £20 million	

Ronnie's been turning defenders inside out with his jaw-dropping tricks for ages! The double FIFA World Player Of The Year wants to prove to everyone that he's still one of the world's top attackers!

franck ribery

Club: Bayern Munich ★ **Age:** 26
Country: France
Value: £60 million

Bundesliga defenders hate it when Ribery charges at them with the ball stuck to his feet! The flying France winger can play on either wing or just behind the strikers, and he's unstoppable in every position!

david silva

Club: Valencia ★ **Age:** 23
Country: Spain
Value: £25 million

When the Mestalla magician has the ball at his feet, no-one knows how to stop him! The lethal left winger has bags of tricks and loves curling deadly balls into the box for David Villa to bury!

robinho

Club: Man. City ★ **Age:** 25
Country: Brazil
Value: £25 million

The most expensive player in British footy history can turn defenders inside out with his silky skills! Robinho's a top trickster who loves getting into the box and ripping the net wide open!

theo walcott

Club: Arsenal ★ **Age:** 20
Country: England
Value: £20 million

One day Walcott will be a central striker like former Arsenal legend Thierry Henry, but right now he's awesome on the wing! Theo's speed with the ball is frightening, and the England star's an ice-cool finisher!

cristiano ronaldo

Club: Real Madrid ★ **Age:** 24
Country: Portugal
Value: £80 million

The FIFA World Player Of The Year can't wait to show everyone why Real smashed the world transfer record to sign him from Man. United! He's big, strong, skilful, great in the air and strikes the ball like a bullet!

WORLD DREAM TEAM!
strikers!

alexandre pato
Club: AC Milan ★ **Age:** 20
Country: Brazil
Value: £30 million

AC's wonderkid has been scoring goals for fun since he arrived from Internacional in 2007 – and he's still only 20 years old! The young Brazil star wants to fire Milan to their first Serie A title since 2004!

sergio aguero
Club: Atletico Madrid ★ **Age:** 21
Country: Argentina
Value: £45 million

Loads of top clubs have been checking out Atletico's mega young striker after he netted 17 goals in 2008-09! He loves using his power to hold off defenders, then drill the ball into the back of the net!

didier drogba
Club: Chelsea ★ **Age:** 31
Country: Ivory Coast
Value: £20 million

Drog is one of the toughest strikers on the planet to mark – defenders must hate trying to stop him! The ace hitman bullies centre-backs with his strength and has one of the hardest shots in world footy!

zlatan ibrahimovic
Club: Barcelona ★ **Age:** 27
Country: Sweden
Value: £60 million

Zlatan fired Inter Milan to the Serie A title last season, then bagged a mega move to Barça! The giant target man is one of the most skilful players on the planet and isn't afraid to shoot from anywhere!

fernando torres
Club: Liverpool ★ **Age:** 25
Country: Spain
Value: £40 million

In just over two Prem seasons, El Nino has shown everyone why he's one of the most feared strikers on the planet! He uses awesome acceleration to burst through defences and his right foot rocks!

wayne rooney

Club: Man. United ★ **Age:** 23
Country: England
Value: £40 million

Now Cristiano Ronaldo has moved to Spain, Man. United fans need Rooney to unleash his scoring talent on the Prem! The England striker never stops running and is a deadly one-on-one finisher!

samuel eto'o

Club: Inter Milan ★ **Age:** 28
Country: Cameroon
Value: £25 million

The new star of Serie A is one of the greatest strikers of the last decade! Cameroon's penalty-box poacher scored over 25 goals in three different seasons for Spanish giants Barcelona!

edin dzeko

Club: Wolfsburg ★ **Age:** 23
Country: Bosnia & Herzegovina
Value: £20 million

Wolfsburg shocked the Bundesliga by winning the title in 2009, and it was all thanks to Dzeko! The giant striker showed Germany's defenders what he's made of by slamming in 26 league goals!

thierry henry

Club: Barcelona ★ **Age:** 32
Country: France
Value: £14 million

Henry hit back at critics who thought he was past his best by bagging 25 goals for Barça last season! The France striker still has pace to burn and gives goalkeepers no chance with his lethal finishing!

david villa

Club: Valencia ★ **Age:** 27
Country: Spain
Value: £40 million

Loads of top European clubs have been chasing Villa since he scored 28 goals in La Liga last season! 'The Kid' is electric around the penalty area – if he gets an inch of space, he usually hits the net!

MATCH'S WORLD DREAM TEAM!
check out our best starting line-up!

casillas

maicon

vidic

ferdinand

clichy

messi

kaka

gerrard

ronaldo

torres

rooney

IF YOU THINK YOU CAN PICK A BETTER DREAM TEAM, FILL IN YOUR FAVE LINE-UP ON THE OPPOSITE PAGE!

PICK YOUR WORLD DREAM TEAM!

now choose your all-star mega team!

WRITE IN THE NAMES OF YOUR FAVE STARTING XI AND SEND IT TO THE ADDRESS BELOW!

goalkeeper
Petr cech

right-back
Sagna

centre-back
NVidic

centre-back
rFerdinand

left-back
r carvalho

right-wing
T wallcott

central-midfield
Ronaldinho

central-midfield
Robinho

left-wing
A arshevin

striker
Ronaldo

striker
d berbatov

SEND YOUR TEAM TO:
MY WORLD DREAM TEAM, MATCH MAGAZINE, MEDIA HOUSE, LYNCHWOOD, PETERBOROUGH, PE2 6EA.

IF YOU DON'T WANT TO CUT UP YOUR MATCH ANNUAL, JUST PHOTOCOPY THIS PAGE!

CLASSIC MOMENTS OF 2009!

No.2

THRILLER BEATS VILLA!

![MAN. UTD]	**MAN. UNITED**	**3**
	Ronaldo 14, 80, Macheda 90	
![AVFC]	**ASTON VILLA**	**2**
	Carew 30, Agbonlahor 58	

Date: April 5

Stadium: Old Trafford, Manchester

Competition: Premier League

What happened? After Liverpool's last-gasp winner against Fulham the day before, United needed three points against Villa to climb back to the top of the table, but they were 2-1 down with ten minutes left! Cristiano Ronaldo fired a low shot into the corner to pull his side level, before 17-year-old striker Federico Macheda came off the bench to curl a stunning winner into the corner from 18 yards on his debut!

NAME THE TEAM!

WHO STARTED FOR MAN. UNITED AGAINST BARÇA IN THE CHAMPIONS LEAGUE FINAL?

2 DEFENDER N Vidic

4 FULL-BACK J oshea

6 STRIKER RONALDO

1 GOALKEEPER E Vandersar

3 DEFENDER R Ferdinand

5 MIDFIELDER Anderson

7 MIDFIELDER

8 MIDFIELDER ANSWER

9 WINGER ANSWER

10 FULL-BACK ANSWER

11 WINGER ANSWER

4 POINTS FOR EACH CORRECT ANSWER!

MY SCORE /40

SPOT THE DIFFERENCE!

CAN YOU FIND THE TEN DIFFERENCES BETWEEN THESE TWO TOP FOOTY PICS?

1 POINT FOR EACH CORRECT ANSWER!

MY SCORE /10

ANSWERS - PAGES 90-91!

HeROes

2009

cristiano ronaldo

DRAW THE OF THE FUTURE!

DESIGN ME SOME COOL NEW BOOTS!

We want you to design the flash new boots of the future! Just use the blank boot on the right-hand page to create a cool design, then send it to the address at the bottom of the page. If you don't want to wreck your Annual, just send us a photocopy. We'll put the best design in a future issue of MATCH and the winner bags a pair of Nike CTR360 boots from our mates at Pro-Direct. To get you started, we've come up with three crazy examples below...

CRAZY COLOURS!

SECRET WEAPONS!

ARMOUR-PLATED!

BOOTS WIN!

WIN AN AWESOME NEW PAIR OF NIKE BOOTS!

MY FUTURE BOOTS!

PRO-DIRECT
www.prodirectsoccer.com

BOOT NAME:

WHY THEY'RE COOL:

MY NAME:

MY ADDRESS:

MY AGE:

Send your drawing to: **Future Boots Competition, MATCH Magazine, Media House, Lynchwood, Peterborough, PE2 6EA.**

BIG TEN!

CAN YOU ANSWER THESE TEN TRICKY QUESTIONS ABOUT AWESOME CHAMPIONSHIP FOOTY?

1 Who is the captain of Nottingham Forest?

2 Which Premier League club did Sheffield United sign Ched Evans From?

3 In which stadium do Ipswich Town play their home games?

4 True or False? Derby manager Nigel Clough's dad won the English League title with The Rams!

5 What is the nickname of Championship new boys Peterborough?

6 Which Prem club did Cardiff sign goal machine Michael Chopra From last summer?

7 What country does Middlesbrough defender Emanuel Pogatetz play For?

8 This wicked wonderkid joined Crystal Palace on loan From West Ham For the season! Who is he?

9 Which League 1 club did Leicester hero Matty Fryatt start his career with – Swindon, Walsall or Southend?

10 Which Premier League club splashed out £5 million on Former Cardiff defender Roger Johnson in July 2009?

5 POINTS FOR EACH CORRECT ANSWER!

MY SCORE /50

ANSWERS - PAGES 90-91!

HEROES

factfile!

age: 29

club: Liverpool

position: Midfielder

value: £40 million

country: England

footy fact! The Liverpool captain has scored in the Champions League, FA Cup, League Cup and UEFA Cup finals! What a legend!

2009

steven gerrard

HERE COMES THE...
WORLD CUP!

TOP TEAMS!

For the first time ever the World Cup will be played in Africa, with a massive 32 teams battling it out to lift the famous trophy! Hosts South Africa, Australia and Holland were some of the first teams to qualify!

MEET ZAKUMI!

The mascot for World Cup 2010 is a leopard called Zakumi! The 'Za' part of his name stands for South Africa, and 'Kumi' means 'ten'! The wicked leopard has crazy green hair to symbolise a footy pitch!

DRAW DAY!

The draw for the World Cup group stages takes place in Cape Town on December 4! Eight groups of four countries will be picked, with the hosts South Africa in Group A!

Soccer City Stadium

DON'T FORGET THESE DATES!

Group Stages	June 11-25
Last 16	June 26-29
Quarter-Finals	July 2-3
Semi-Finals	July 6-7
Final	July 11

MEGA MATCHES!

After a big opening ceremony, South Africa will play the World Cup's first match on June 11 in the ace Soccer City Stadium in Johannesburg! There will be two live games on TV every day during the group stages!

THE HOSTS!

WHAT HAPPENED AT...
WORLD CUP 2006?

GERMAN PARTY!

The last World Cup was held in Germany, the second time they'd hosted the tournament! They came close to the final, but lost 2-0 to Italy in the semis when Fabio Grosso and Alessandro Del Piero hit late goals!

FAB FOUR!

Italy won the World Cup for the fourth time after beating France 5-3 on penalties in the 2006 final! Zinedine Zidane put France 1-0 up, but he was then sent off for headbutting Marco Materazzi in the chest!

SUPER STRIKER!

Even though Germany didn't reach the 2006 final, lethal hitman Miroslav Klose won the Golden Boot! The Bayern Munich star scored five goals, including a brace in the opening match against Costa Rica!

PENALTY AGONY!

England's terrible record in penalty shoot-outs continued as they lost in the quarter-finals in 2006! After Wayne Rooney was sent off, the Three Lions went down 3-1 on spot-kicks to Portugal!

SOUTH AFRICA

SOCCER CITY STADIUM

①

JOHANNESBURG
CAPACITY: 94,700

FAB FACT: Soccer City Stadium will host the tournament's opening match on June 11, and the final a month later!

GREEN POINT STADIUM

②

CAPE TOWN
CAPACITY: 70,000

FAB FACT: This wicked World Cup stadium is built right next to the Atlantic Ocean! It's awesome!

DURBAN STADIUM

③

DURBAN
CAPACITY: 70,000

FAB FACT: This flash footy ground has a giant arch stretching over the roof, just like Wembley!

ELLIS PARK STADIUM

④

JOHANNESBURG
CAPACITY: 61,000

FAB FACT: The final of the 2009 Confederations Cup was played here, when Brazil beat the USA 3-2!

FREE STATE STADIUM

⑤

BLOEMFONTEIN
CAPACITY: 48,000

FAB FACT: This ground is home to Bloemfontein Celtic – one of the richest clubs in the South Africa Premiership!

NELSON MANDELA BAY STADIUM

⑥

PORT ELIZABETH
CAPACITY: 48,000

FAB FACT: This class stadium is named after Nelson Mandela, who was South Africa's president from 1994 to 1999!

Map of South Africa showing stadium locations: Pietersburg (9), Pretoria (8, 7, 4, 1), (10), Bloemfontein (5), Durban (3), Cape Town (2), (6). SOUTH AFRICA.

LOFTUS VERSFELD STADIUM

⑦

PRETORIA
CAPACITY: 50,000

FAB FACT: The home stadium of the Mamelodi Sundowns was first used for sport way back in 1903!

ROYAL BAFOKENG STADIUM

⑧

RUSTENBURG
CAPACITY: 42,000

FAB FACT: The smallest stadium for World Cup 2010 hosted four matches at last summer's Confederations Cup!

PETER MOKABA STADIUM

⑨

POLOKWANE
CAPACITY: 46,000

FAB FACT: Polokwane is home to the country's famous upside-down tree, the Boabab. It's the biggest tree in Africa!

MBOMBELA STADIUM

⑩

NELSPRUIT
CAPACITY: 46,000

FAB FACT: The wicked stadium's name, Mbombela, means 'many people together in a small space'!

10 THINGS YOU DIDN'T KNOW ABOUT...
THE WORLD CUP!

1 The World Cup is being played in Africa for the first time in 2010! It's been held in Europe ten times!

2 The World Cup trophy weighs just 6.175kg! FIFA saw 53 designs before picking one by top Italian artist Silvio Gazzaniga!

3 England's biggest TV audience for a World Cup match was against Argentina in 2002, when 450 million tuned in!

4 Brazil's legendary Maracana stadium in Rio de Janeiro will host the World Cup final for a second time in 2014!

5 Italy's *Gennaro Gattuso* is just one of two bearded players to win the World Cup! The other was Argentina's *Sergio Batista* in 1986!

6 Italy's World Cup-winning skipper *Fabio Cannavaro* bagged his 100th international cap in the 2006 final in Germany!

7 Brazil have won the World Cup five times! Italy are second on the list with four victories, while England have lifted the trophy once!

8 The 2,000th goal in World Cup history was scored against England by Sweden's Marcus Allback in 2006!

9 England have never won a World Cup penalty shoot-out! Together with Italy, they've lost on spot-kicks three times!

10 The fastest World Cup goal was scored by Turkey star *Hakan Sükür* after 11 seconds against South Korea in 2002!

CHAMPO

CHELSEA	4
Drogba 52, Alex 57, Lampard 76, 89	

LIVERPOOL	4
Aurelio 19, Alonso 28, Lucas 81, Kuyt 82	

Date: April 14

Stadium: Stamford Bridge, London

Competition: Champions League quarter-final

What happened? Chelsea looked to be cruising into the Champions League semi-finals after a 3-1 first leg win at Anfield, but Liverpool had other ideas! A Fabio Aurelio free-kick and a Xabi Alonso penalty pulled The Reds level on aggregate by half-time, but Chelsea stormed back as Didier Drogba, an unstoppable Alex free-kick and a Frank Lampard brace bagged a 7-5 aggregate win and a semi-final place!

CLASSIC!

MATT TAYLOR...

ON THE SPOT!

MATCH ASKS BOLTON'S GOALSCORING MIDFIELDER ALL THE BIG QUESTIONS!

> THOSE QUESTIONS WERE A BIT TRICKY, MATCH!

RONALDO OR MESSI?

TAYLOR SAYS: "Definitely Ronaldo! I reckon he's the best player I've played against in my career!"

NIGHT IN OR NIGHT OUT?

TAYLOR SAYS: "A night in with the missus. My mate gets me all the latest DVDs, so I've always got loads to watch!"

BASKETBALL OR AMERICAN FOOTBALL?

TAYLOR SAYS: "If I had to choose one of them, I'd say I probably prefer watching American Football!"

SHOPPING OR CINEMA?

TAYLOR SAYS: "I actually don't mind going shopping, so I'll say that. I love buying new jeans with the missus!"

PIZZA OR PIE?

TAYLOR SAYS: "That's a tough one, MATCH! I think pizzas are probably just a little bit better, though!"

"RONALDO'S THE BEST PLAYER I'VE EVER PLAYED AGAINST!"

FEDERER OR NADAL?

TAYLOR SAYS: "I like Rafael Nadal, but it's got to be Roger Federer. He's on a different level to everyone else!"

HEROES

2009

lionel messi

DAVID BECKHAM'S

MATCH CHECKS OUT THE CAREER OF ENGLAND'S FREE-KICK KING!

MAY 1992: YOUTH CUP WINNER!

Becks won the FA Youth Cup with Man. United team-mates Nicky Butt and Gary Neville, and scored in the second leg of the Final!

DECEMBER 1994: CHAMPO LEAGUE DEBUT!

He made his first European appearance in a 4-0 win against Galatasary, and got on the scoresheet!

FEBRUARY 1995: PRESTON LOAN!

Becks played five games on loan at Preston in 1995 and scored twice - one was direct from a corner!

APRIL 1995: PREM DEBUT!

The young Man. United midfielder made his first appearance in the top flight in a goalless draw against Leeds!

SCRAPBOOK!

**AUGUST 1995:
FIRST UNITED GOAL!**

Man. United lost their First game of 1995-96 to Aston Villa, but Becks scored in the 3-1 defeat!

**MARCH 1996:
WICKED WINNER!**

Beckham buried the winner against Chelsea in the 1996 FA Cup semi-final at Villa Park!

**MAY 1996:
FA CUP KING!**

Eric Cantona scored From a Becks corner to seal a 1-0 win against Liverpool in the 1996 FA Cup Final!

**AUGUST 1996:
WIMBLEDON WONDER GOAL!**

The First day of the 1996-97 Premier League season saw Dave rip the net From inside his own half at Selhurst Park!

**SEPTEMBER 1996:
FIRST ENGLAND CAP!**

In Glenn Hoddle's First match as manager, Becks made his Three Lions debut against Moldova in a World Cup qualifier! England won 3-0!

STAR OF THE SHOW!

The England hero then signed mega advertising deals with Pepsi, Police shades and Brylcreem!

BECKS' SCRAPBOOK!

JUNE 1998: FIRST ENGLAND GOAL!

Beckham made his World Cup debut against Colombia at France '98 and scored with a stunning free-kick!

JUNE 1998: WORLD CUP PAIN!

He was then sent off for kicking Argentina's Diego Simeone as England were knocked out of the World Cup on penalties!

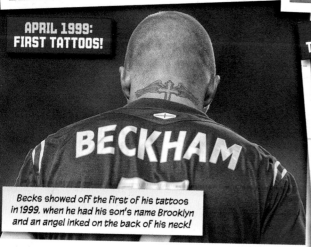

APRIL 1999: FIRST TATTOOS!

Becks showed off the first of his tattoos in 1999, when he had his son's name Brooklyn and an angel inked on the back of his neck!

MAY 1999: TREBLE TIME!

The midfield ace won the treble with United, and set up both goals as they stormed back to beat Bayern Munich in the Champions League Final!

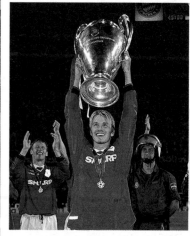

NOVEMBER 2000: ENGLAND SKIPPER!

Caretaker boss Peter Taylor handed Becks the captain's armband for the first time in a friendly against Italy!

OCTOBER 2001: WORLD CUP TIME!

An awesome Beckham free-kick in stoppage time against Greece at Old Trafford sealed England's place at World Cup 2002!

JUNE 2002: SPOT-KICK KING!

Becks was doubtful for the World Cup after breaking his foot, but he battled back to get revenge for 1998 by scoring a winning penalty against Argentina!

JULY 2003: BERNABEU BOUND!

After 263 Prem appearances and six titles, Becks joined Real Madrid for £25 million!

JUNE 2006: SKIPPER STEPS DOWN!

After scoring against Ecuador in the second round of World Cup 2006, England crashed out against Portugal and Becks resigned as captain!

JUNE 2004: EURO EXIT!

He led England to the Euro 2004 quarter-finals, but saw his penalty sail over the bar as England lost a shoot-out against Portugal!

JULY 2007: HEADING TO LA!

After four seasons in Spain, Becks moved to LA Galaxy! He won his only La Liga title in his last game for Real!

MARCH 2008: ENGLAND CENTURY!

He then became only the fifth player to win 100 England caps in a friendly against France in Paris!

JANUARY 2009: SAN SIRO SWITCH!

Beckham returned to Europe to wear the No.32 shirt for AC Milan in a loan move, and scored two goals in his first four games!

MARCH 2009: RECORD BREAKER!

The England legend broke Bobby Moore's record of 108 caps by an outfield player as he played his 109th game in a friendly against Slovakia!

CRAZY HAIRCUTS!

CHECK OUT SOME OF BECKS' MAD STYLES!

LONG & GREASY!

RUBBISH CURTAINS!

MINGIN' MOHICAN!

GIRLY PONYTAIL!

DODGY BRAIDS!

WICKED WORDSEARCH!

FIND ALL TEN PREM NEW BOYS IN THIS MEGA GRID!

```
K M K U R U C Z Q E K R O O R G C W G C
N B P V A C P O G B F G X P R I L Y X Q
Q W T A N U T S X N P V J Y W D F T P S
P C B E J W R K E R D P A Q Z G E A F M
A U G O S V Z L U U H C P U H Z R Q Y T
Q E O R I G E V O C Y H C A N A G U U U
G I A N N A K O P O U L O S M I U I X K
E E V B M V I H T S J E I H K Q S L Y Y
M A D R I L S E S P I N O Z A O O A Y B
T V E N G A Q Q M L X N A O P S N N W K
O V I Z H I R K O V L T M Z V T E I G R
O E Q Q L D Z K U S Z E B E N I T E Z I
O N L F H R P A Q N P D A G X U O E F V
G D P Q U P N M B A L I J K K B P A U C
M Y F P I T Q S R P G L L B F M G A V Q
```

Aquilani
Benitez
Cana
Espinoza
Ferguson
Giannakopoulos
Kurucz
Mears
Vermaelen
Zhirkov

3 POINTS FOR EACH CORRECT ANSWER!

MY SCORE /30

PART-TIME PROS!

WHICH PREMIER LEAGUE LEGENDS HAVE FOUND THEMSELVES CRAZY NEW JOBS?

4 POINTS FOR EACH CORRECT ANSWER!

MY SCORE /20

1. This Arsenal speed machine would be the world's fastest postman!

T Walcott

2. Which Chelsea star is ready to start working on a farm to earn more cash?

D Drogba

3. Which Liverpool and England defender wants to blast off to the moon?

G Johnson

4. Which Man. United hitman looks like he'd make a rubbish pirate?

D berbatov

5. This Man. City hero looks like he's already bored of fixing cars!

C Tevez

ANSWERS - PAGES 90-91!

HEROES

2009

ronaldinho

With his master tactics, the England manager is great at unlocking the meanest defences! Not sure about the green suit, though!

I'M SACKING MY AGENT RIGHT NOW!

I'M NOT HAPPY ABOUT THIS!

RONALDO WOULD BE...
PIKACHU

Real Madrid's wicked £80 million star causes opponents loads of trouble, just like the electric attacks of the ace Pokémon character!

IF FOOTY STARS WeRe...
GAME He

THIS IS NOT COOL!

JERMAIN DEFOE WOULD BE...
YOSHI

The Spurs and England goal machine has loads of pace and loves to gobble up defenders, just like Mario's mate!

GARETH BARRY WOULD BE...
SOLID SNAKE

The Man. City
midfielder uses his
stealth skills to stop
enemy attacks, just like
the rock-solid soldier
from Metal Gear
Solid!

CAN
I USE THIS
KIT TO PLAY
MATCHES?

DAVID BECKHAM WOULD BE...
MARIO

When he's not
playing football,
England legend
Becks loves nothing
better than burning
around in all his
flash motors!

THINK
I PREFER
MY ASTON
MARTIN TO
THIS!

ROES!

WHO
WANTS TO
MESS WITH
ME?

THEO WALCOTT WOULD BE...
SONIC THE HEDGEHOG

Theo and Sonic
have one main thing
in common – they're
both lightning fast!
When they hit top
speed, you'll never
catch them!

WHO
STOLE MY
PANTS?

DIDIER DROGBA WOULD BE...
MASTER CHIEF

The Drog's
monster strength
scares the life out of
everyone he faces, just
like the one-man army
from the awesome
Halo games!

MOMENTS OF 2009!

No.4

ANDREY

LIVERPOOL	**4**
Torres 49, 72, Benayoun 56, 90	

ARSENAL	**4**
Arshavin 36, 67, 70, 90	

Date: April 21

Stadium: Anfield, Liverpool

Competition: Premier League

What happened? Arsenal's record signing Andrey Arshavin became the first player in Prem history to net four goals in a match and still not win! A week after Liverpool had drawn 4-4 against Chelsea in the Champions League, the electric Russian playmaker dealt their Prem title challenge a massive blow as he became the first opposition player to hit four goals in a league match at Anfield since 1946!

HITS FOUR!

BIG TEN!

ANSWER THESE TEN TOUGH QUESTIONS TO PROVE YOU KNOW YOUR SPANISH FOOTY!

1 Name this Real Madrid and France goal king!

ATHLETIC CLUB BILBAO

2 What shirt number does skill machine Lionel Messi wear For Barcelona?

3 What position does Barcelona superstar Daniel Alves play?

4 Which club does ex-Celtic hero Shunsuke Nakamura play For – Sevilla or Espanyol?

5 True or False? Athletic Bilbao have never been relegated From the top Flight!

6 What is Atletico Madrid's nickname – Los Che or The Mattress Makers?

7 Which of these clubs has never won the La Liga title – Deportivo La Coruna, Real Betis or Villarreal?

8 Who is the manager of La Liga giants Real Madrid?

9 How old is Barcelona midfielder Andres Iniesta – 24, 25 or 26 years old?

10 Which La Liga team plays its home games at the Riazor stadium?

5 POINTS FOR EACH CORRECT ANSWER!

MY SCORE /50

ANSWERS – PAGES 90-91!

HEROES

2009

emmanuel adebayor

BACK IN

NICKLAS BENDTNER

THAT LOOKS LIKE MY EVIL TWIN SISTER!

2005
ARSENAL

NOW
ARSENAL

MAROUANE FELLAINI

EVEN I THINK THIS AFRO LOOKS BAD!

2007
BELGIUM

NOW
EVERTON

ZLATAN IBRAHIMOVIC

I STILL NEVER SMILE!

2001
AJAX

NOW
SWEDEN

FERNANDO TORRES

I'M BURNING ALL OF MY OLD PHOTO ALBUMS!

2004
ATLETICO MADRID

NOW
LIVERPOOL

TIMe!

CARLOS TEVEZ

2001 ARGENTINA

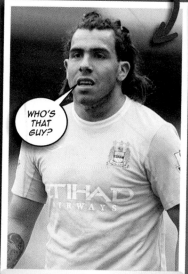

WHO'S THAT GUY?

NOW MAN. CITY

ROB GREEN

2002 NORWICH

I WANT MY HAIR BACK!

NOW WEST HAM

PAUL SCHARNER

2002 AUSTRIA WIEN

PEOPLE LOVE BLUE HAIR IN AUSTRIA!

NOW WIGAN

CRISTIANO RONALDO

2003 SPORTING LISBON

I USED TO SLAP ON SIX TUBS OF GEL IN EVERY MATCH!

NOW REAL MADRID

WADE

BURNLEY	1
Elliott 13	
SHEFFIELD UNITED	0

Date: May 25

Stadium: Wembley, London

Competition: Championship play-off final

What happened? The 2008-09 season was unforgettable for Clarets fans as they watched their side beat Chelsea and Arsenal on their way to the Carling Cup semi-finals, then clinch promotion to the Premier League! Owen Coyle's side's sweetest moment came in the Wembley sunshine as Wade Elliott struck a swerving shot into the top corner to send Burnley back into the top flight for the first time in 33 years!

WINS IT!

WICKED WORDSEARCH!

FIND THE 20 FOREIGN STARS IN THIS MASSIVE GRID!

```
Q L M J I R P Z N S J J I P O I J L B S
G T Z Z F A B R E G A S E H J R E R J A
F W I R R A S G O A P S Q K A T R X F H
I P V J X V E E O I A G C B R P R Q V L
Y T X O S Z A U Q V S A U K O K H W G C
C E E A C V H N G F L Q S E I U D R P N
P V X K R K R O P L B W Y W R N C J E J
Q E B G F S D H A E U T T J A I R X D I
D Z C T V Y H B Z I R O K L G C X R E K
K N C H N N R A W C I S E Q K Q I U R N
T Z I Q H L Q N V H V G I Q J B P O S A
E L M A N D E R C I N R R E F K J B E G
O O D T X V S L X A N C L X S E D F N I
K P T P S K E I H K F H G F S A W E R K
M J N P M M M G W D I L U E W I Z L S F
```

Arshavin
Ballack
Elmander
Fabregas
Hangeland
Melchiot
Pedersen
Skrtel
Tevez
Van Persie

3 POINTS FOR EACH CORRECT ANSWER!

MY SCORE /30

TITLE WINNERS!

10 POINTS FOR EACH CORRECT ANSWER

MY SCORE /20

TWO OF THE AWESOME FOOTY SUPERSTARS BELOW HAVE WON THE PREMIER LEAGUE TITLE! CAN YOU PICK THEM OUT FOR 20 MASSIVE POINTS?

PATRICK VIEIRA ✓

ANDRIY SHEVCHENKO ✓

MICHAEL OWEN ✓

LOUIS SAHA ✓

MATHIEU FLAMINI ✓

ANSWERS - PAGES 90-91!

HEROES

2009

age: 23

club: Man. United

position: Striker

value: £40 million

country: England

footy fact! Man. United's powerhouse striker hit his 100th goal for the club in their 5-0 win against Wigan in August 2009!

wayne rooney

MESSi

ROCKS ROME!

BARCELONA	2
Eto'o 10, Messi 70	
MAN. UNITED	0

Date: May 27

Stadium: Stadio Olimpico, Rome

Competition: Champions League final

What happened? Cristiano Ronaldo's last game in a Man. United shirt ended in heartbreak as Pep Guardiola became the youngest boss to win the Champions League in the heat of the Stadio Olimpico! Samuel Eto'o's near-post strike put the La Liga champions ahead early in the first half, before Lionel Messi brilliantly headed home Barça's second goal from a quality Xavi cross with 20 minutes left on the clock!

BIG TEN!

CAN YOU ANSWER THESE TEN QUESTIONS ABOUT THE AWESOME ENGLAND TEAM?

1 Which country did England Free-kick hero David Beckham win his 100th cap against in 2008?

2 Keeper Joe Hart is spending this season on loan at Birmingham From which Premier League club?

3 Who knocked England out of the 2006 World Cup?

4 Name the England goal machine who scored twice in a Friendly against Holland last August!

5 Which speedy winger made his England debut against Austria in 2007?

6 Which Man. United star scored twice when England crushed Andorra 6-0 in June 2009?

7 Fabio Capello has managed which La Liga club – Barça, Real Madrid or Valencia?

8 How many World Cups has Rio Ferdinand played in?

9 How old is speedy England right-back Glen Johnson – 23, 24 or 25 years old?

10 True or False? MidFielder Steven Gerrard scored his First international goal when England hammered Germany 5-1 in 2001!

5 POINTS FOR EACH CORRECT ANSWER!

MY SCORE /50

ANSWERS – PAGES 90-91!

HEROES

2009

Samuel eto'o

RECORD BREAKERS!

FROM FASTEST GOALS TO TALLEST PLAYERS, **MATCH** CHECKS OUT THE WORLD'S CRAZIEST FOOTY RECORDS!

1.8

Arsenal striker Nicklas Bendtner headed the fastest Prem goal by a sub just 1.8 seconds after coming off the bench against Spurs in 2007!

15,000

Former Fulham defender Moritz Volz smashed in the Prem's 15,000th goal against Chelsea in December 2006!

60

The highest number of goals scored in a top-flight season was 60, by Everton legend Bill 'Dixie' Dean in 1927-28!

11

That's the lowest number of points a team has picked up in a Premier League season, set by Derby's rubbish team in 2007-08!

10

Sheffield United's Keith Gillespie was sent off for elbowing Stephen Hunt just ten seconds after coming off the bench in 2007!

11

That's the most goals scored in a Prem match, when Portsmouth beat Reading 7-4 at Fratton Park in September 2007!

35

Ex-Blackburn striker Alan Shearer holds the record for the most Prem goals in a season! Shearer ripped the net 35 times in 1994-95!

£5.5 MILLION

West Ham were fined £5.5 million for breaking Prem rules when they signed Javier Mascherano and Carlos Tevez in 2006!

43

Former Man. City keeper John Burridge became the Prem's oldest player in 1995 when he played against QPR aged 43!

2

Two red cards have been shown in Champo League finals – to Arsenal's Jens Lehmann in 2006 and Chelsea's Didier Drogba in 2008!

10

The quickest goal scored in the Champions League was by Bayern striker Roy Makaay after ten seconds against Real Madrid in 2007!

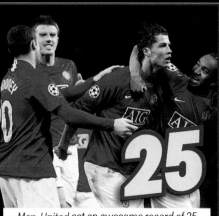

25

Man. United set an awesome record of 25 Champo League games unbeaten – a run that saw them reach the 2008 and 2009 finals!

141

AC Milan legend Paolo Maldini holds the record for the most Champo League games. He played 141 times between 1988 and 2008!

9

Barcelona's Lionel Messi scored the highest number of Champo League goals in 2008-09! Leo bagged nine, including a great header in the final!

123

The latest goal ever scored in the World Cup was by Italy's Alessandro Del Piero in the 123rd minute of their semi-final against Germany in 2006!

3

Clarence Seedorf is the only player to have won the Champions League with three different clubs!

173

Man. United boss Sir Alex Ferguson managed his record-breaking 173rd Champions League game in the 2009 final!

340

The Champo League trophy took a mega 340 hours to make after it was designed by Jürg Stadelmann!

The record for the tallest player in World Cup history goes to Australia keeper Zeljko Kalac!

6FT 8INS

28

Steven Gerrard is Britain's record Euro goalscorer – he netted his 28th Champo League goal in Liverpool's 4-0 win over Real Madrid in 2009!

11,000,000,000

A massive 11 billion people are reported to have watched the 2002 World Cup Final between Brazil and Germany!

4

Russian referee Valentin Ivanov sent off a record four players when Portugal beat Holland 1-0 in the last 16 at World Cup 2006!

15

Brazil legend Ronaldo holds the record for the most World Cup goals. He hit the net 15 times!

5

Germany's Miroslav Klose won the World Cup Golden Boot in 2006 with five goals!

3

The only player to score a World Cup final hat-trick is England's Sir Geoff Hurst in 1966!

DREAM TEAM!

CAN YOU WORK OUT WHICH PREM STARS HAVE BEEN PICKED IN THIS ACE LINE-UP?

Wigan's No.1 – CK!

GK

ANSWER

Aston Villa's Senegal star – HB!

RB

ANSWER

Man. City's ex-Gunner – KT!

CB

ANSWER

Prem's tallest defender – ZK!

CB

ANSWER

Chelsea & England star – AC!

LB

ANSWER

Arsenal's wicked captain!

RM

CESC FABREGAS

Everton's midfield ace – TC!

CM

ANSWER

Stoke's long-throw king!

CM

ANSWER

Spurs' Croatia hero – LM!

LM

ANSWER

West Ham's on-loan Inter star!

S

ANSWER

Sunderland's £10 million man!

S

ANSWER

3 POINTS FOR EACH CORRECT ANSWER!	
MY SCORE	/30

STADIUM GAME!

MATCH THESE COOL STADIUMS TO THE CLASS CLUBS THAT PLAY IN THEM!

ALLIANZ ARENA	STADE VELODROME	SIGNAL IDUNA PARK	LA BOMBONERA	STADIO OLIMPICO
1	2	3	4	5

A	B	C	D	e
ROMA	BOCA JUNIORS	BORUSSIA DORTMUND	BAYERN MUNICH	MARSEILLE

4 POINTS FOR EACH CORRECT ANSWER!	
MY SCORE	/20

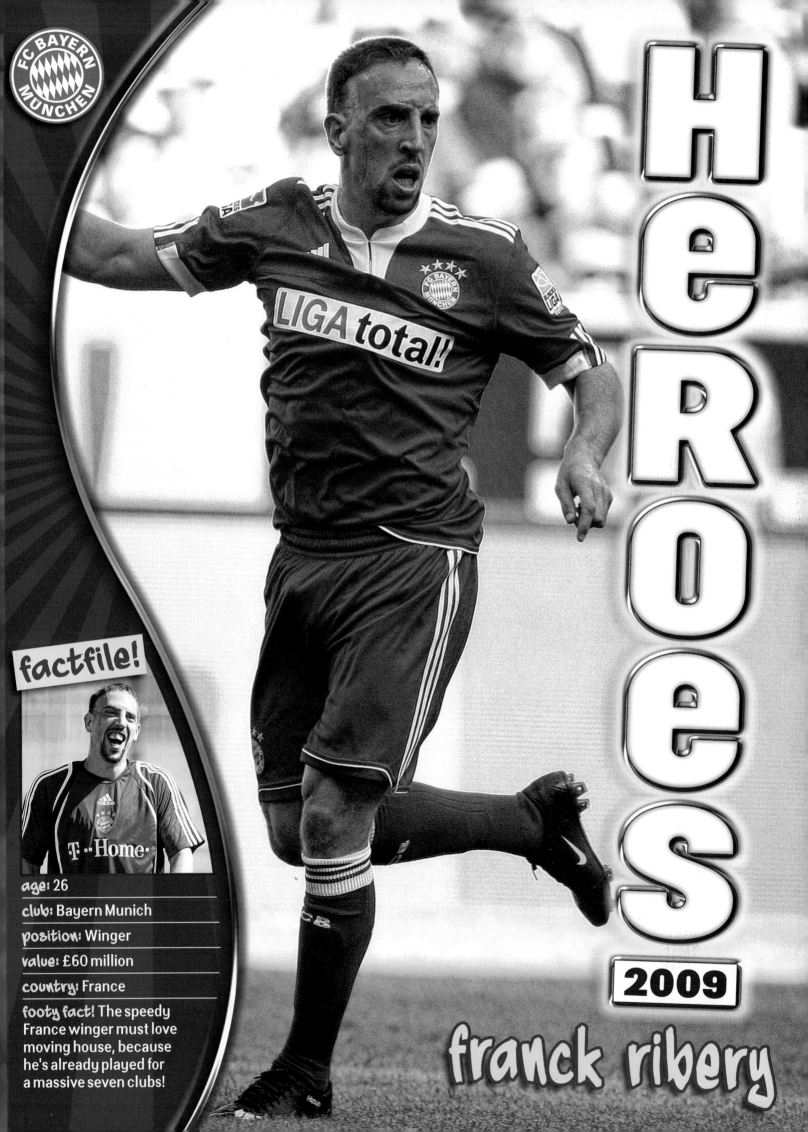

FC BAYERN MUNCHEN

HEROES

factfile!

age: 26

club: Bayern Munich

position: Winger

value: £60 million

country: France

footy fact! The speedy France winger must love moving house, because he's already played for a massive seven clubs!

LIGA total!

2009

franck ribery

CLASSIC MOMENTS OF 2009! No.7

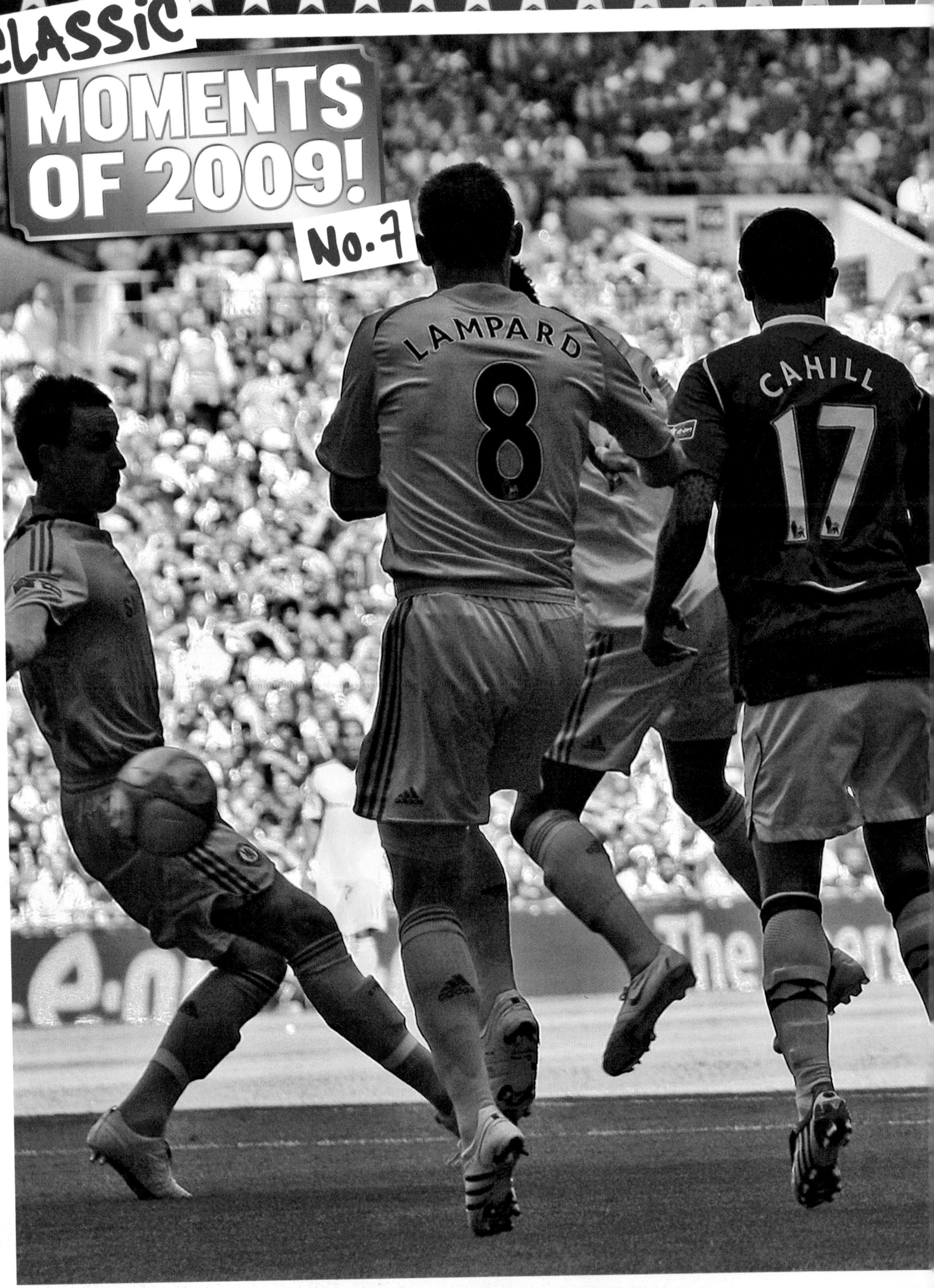

CUP KINGS!

CHELSEA	**2**
Drogba 21, Lampard 72	

EVERTON	**1**
Saha 1	

Date: May 30

Stadium: Wembley, London

Competition: FA Cup final

What happened? Not one, but two FA Cup records were set in the 2009 final! Everton striker Louis Saha wrote his name into the history books with the fastest ever final goal after just 25 seconds, but The Toffees couldn't hold out as a Didier Drogba header and a Frank Lampard screamer won the trophy for Chelsea. Blues left-back Ashley Cole then picked up his record-equalling fifth winners' medal!

10

THE DINOSAUR
HAMBURG
The wicked Bundesliga club is known as 'The Dinosaur' because it's been around for ages! Hamburg formed in 1887 and have been playing in the German top flight since 1963!

9

THE PHANTOM
ROY MAKAAY
The deadly Dutch striker picked up his scary nickname because he's so good at scoring goals out of nothing! Makaay's bagged over 300 goals in his 16-year career!

8

THE MATTRESS MAKERS
ATLETICO MADRID
Spanish giants Atletico Madrid have loads of top stars like Diego Forlan and Sergio Aguero, but they've got a weird nickname! People reckon their red and white home shirts look like old-fashioned mattresses!

7

THE SHRIMPERS
SOUTHEND UNITED
Most fans call League 1 club Southend 'The Blues', but they're also known as 'The Shrimpers'! It's a tribute to the seaside town's famous fishing industry!

6

THE DUCK
ALEXANDRE PATO
The AC Milan wonderkid has a rubbish nickname, but he's a top striker! The speedy Brazil hitman netted 15 goals as Milan bagged a Champions League place in 2008-09!

5

THE BISON
MICHAEL ESSIEN
Chelsea's box-to-box midfielder is a Premier League legend! The Ghana international earned his nickname because of his tough tackling in the middle of the park!

SOUTHEND UNITED

MATCH COUNTS DOWN THE FUNNIEST FOOTY NAMES OF ALL TIME!

4

THE YELLOW SUBMARINE
VILLARREAL
The La Liga club picked up this crazy name because of their yellow home kit! The club's mascot, Little Yellow, watches every home game and has a submarine on his head!

THE CAT
IKER CASILLAS
Real Madrid keeper Casillas makes so many unreal saves that people think he's as agile as a cat! Fans call him 'Il Gato', which means 'The Cat', because he prowls around his area keeping loads of clean sheets!

3

2

THE MONKEY HANGERS
HARTLEPOOL UNITED
The League 1 club are known as the 'Monkey Hangers', because some locals in the town hanged a monkey that they thought was a French spy in the 1800s! United's mascot is even called H'Angus!

1

THE WARDROBE
PAPA BOUBA DIOP
Check out this awesome nickname! Because he's so massive, the wicked Portsmouth and Senegal midfielder was named after a piece of furniture when he used to play for Fulham!

BIG TEN!

HOW MUCH DO YOU KNOW ABOUT ITALIAN FOOTY?
TEST YOURSELF WITH THESE QUESTIONS!

1 Name this awesome AC Milan defender!

2 True or False? Juventus midfielder Momo Sissoko has won the FA Cup!

3 Which Udinese forward is also the club captain?

4 What country does wicked Roma left-back John Arne Riise play for?

5 Which Serie A club did Fiorentina sign Alberto Gilardino from?

6 Which club finished fifth in Serie A in 2008-09?

7 Who scored more goals in Serie A last season - Francesco Totti or Alexandre Pato?

8 Which club was promoted to Italy's top flight after finishing as champions of Serie B in 2008-09?

9 How many goals did David Beckham score while on loan at AC Milan in 2008-09 - two, three or five?

10 When Inter Milan signed Samuel Eto'o from Barcelona, which striker moved to the Nou Camp?

5 POINTS FOR EACH CORRECT ANSWER!

MY SCORE /50

ANSWERS - PAGES 90-91!

HEROES

2009

didier drogba

factfile!

age: 31

club: Chelsea

position: Striker

value: £20 million

country: Ivory Coast

footy fact! Drogba always seems to save his best form for big games – he's scored in five major English cup finals for The Blues!

MEGA WORLD TRANSFERS!

MATCH CHECKS OUT THE BIGGEST MOVES IN FOOTY HISTORY!

10

DIMITAR BERBATOV
FEE: £30.75 MILLION
FROM: Tottenham
TO: Man. United

After 27 goals in 70 Prem matches, Man. United paid mega money for Berba - nearly three times what Spurs spent on the Bulgaria striker in 2006!

9

ANDRIY SHEVCHENKO
FEE: £30.8 MILLION
FROM: AC Milan
TO: Chelsea

Chelsea broke the British transfer record to sign the Ukraine striker in 2006, but Sheva only managed to score nine goals in 48 Prem games!

8

CHRISTIAN VIERI

FEE: £31 MILLION

FROM: Lazio
TO: Inter Milan

Inter smashed the world record to sign Vieri from Lazio in 1999! The Italian goal king hit 46 goals in just 48 league matches in 2002 and 2003!

7

ROBINHO

FEE: £32.5 MILLION

FROM: Real Madrid
TO: Man. City

City snapped up the Brazilian trickster on the last day of the summer transfer window in 2008, and Robi fired home 14 goals in his debut Prem season!

CLUB BY CLUB!
Check out your fave team's biggest buy!

ARSENAL
ANDREY ARSHAVIN
FEE: £15 MILLION

ASTON VILLA
STEWART DOWNING
FEE: £12 MILLION

BIRMINGHAM
CHRISTIAN BENITEZ
FEE: £8.5 MILLION

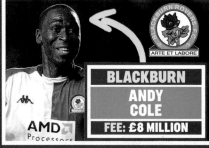

BLACKBURN
ANDY COLE
FEE: £8 MILLION

BOLTON
JOHAN ELMANDER
FEE: £11 MILLION

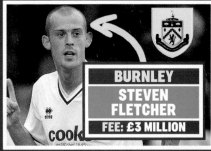

BURNLEY
STEVEN FLETCHER
FEE: £3 MILLION

CHELSEA
ANDRIY SHEVCHENKO
FEE: £30.8 MILLION

EVERTON
MARQUANE FELLAINI
FEE: £15 MILLION

FULHAM
STEVE MARLET
FEE: £11.5 MILLION

HULL
JIMMY BULLARD
FEE: £5 MILLION

LIVERPOOL
FERNANDO TORRES
FEE: £26.5 MILLION

MAN. CITY
ROBINHO
FEE: £32.5 MILLION

MAN. UNITED
DIMITAR BERBATOV
FEE: £30.75 MILLION

PORTSMOUTH
PETER CROUCH
FEE: £11 MILLION

6

GIANLUIGI BUFFON
FEE: £32.6 MILLION
FROM: Parma
TO: Juventus

Juventus splashed out big money to sign Buffon in 2001, and he's since won two Serie A titles and helped Italy lift the World Cup in 2006!

5

HERNAN CRESPO
FEE: £35.5 MILLION
FROM: Parma
TO: Lazio

Crespo never really showed his best form during his time with Chelsea, but he was deadly in Italy! He was Serie A's top scorer with 26 goals in 2001!

4

LUIS FIGO

FEE: £37.5 MILLION

FROM: Barcelona
TO: Real Madrid

The Portugal playmaker won two La Liga titles with Barça, then joined their massive rivals in 2000 and was named World Player Of The Year in 2001!

3

ZINEDINE ZIDANE

FEE: £47.2 MILLION

FROM: Juventus
TO: Real Madrid

Real broke the world record to sign the double World Player Of The Year in 2001, and he hit the winner in the Champo League final just a year later!

STOKE
DAVE KITSON
FEE: £5.5 MILLION

SUNDERLAND
CRAIG GORDON
FEE: £9 MILLION

TOTTENHAM
DARREN BENT
FEE: £16.5 MILLION

WEST HAM
SAVIO
FEE: £9 MILLION

WIGAN
CHARLES N'ZOGBIA
FEE: £6 MILLION

WOLVES
KEVIN DOYLE
FEE: £6.5 MILLION

CHECK OUT MATCH EVERY WEEK FOR BIG TRANSFER GOSSIP!

2

1

CRISTIANO RONALDO

FEE: £80 MILLION

FROM: Man. United
TO: Real Madrid

Just days after signing Kaka, Real smashed the world record again to bag the flying Portugal winger! We've heard Ronaldo's earning £200,000-a-week!

EVERTON	1
Saha 90	

ARSENAL	6
Denilson 26, Vermaelen 37, Gallas 41, Fabregas 48, 69, Eduardo 89	

Date: August 15

Stadium: Goodison Park, Liverpool

Competition: Premier League

What happened? Arsenal fans were expecting a tough trip to Goodison on the opening day of the 2009-10 season, but they watched their side destroy a shell-shocked Everton team in a one-sided game! Denilson opened the scoring with a 25-yard rocket, and the game was over before half-time when Gallas and Vermaelen both headed home. A Cesc Fabregas brace and a late Eduardo strike completed the rout!

TOFFEES HIT FOR SIX!

MATCHY'S QUIZ!

HOW DID YOU GET ON WITH MY TOUGH FOOTY QUIZZES?

NAME THE TEAM!

1. Edwin van der Sar; 2. Nemanja Vidic;
3. Rio Ferdinand; 4. John O'Shea; 5. Anderson;
6. Ryan Giggs; 7. Michael Carrick; 8. Wayne
Rooney; 9. Patrice Evra; 10. Ji-Sung Park.

MY SCORE: /30

SPOT THE DIFFERENCE!

1. Fernando Torres has lost his hair; 2. Fernando
Torres' right boot is missing; 3. Fernando Torres'
left boot is missing; 4. Fernando Torres' shorts
are now No.22; 5. Dirk Kuyt's shirt sponsor is
now 'Liverpool'; 6. The fan's shirt is now yellow;
7. The band on Curtis Davies' left sock is now red;
8. Curtis Davies' left arm is missing; 9. The
number on Dirk Kuyt's shorts is missing;
10. The badge on Nicky Shorey's shirt is missing.

MY SCORE: /20

BIG TEN – CHAMPIONSHIP!

1. Paul McKenna; 2. Man. City; 3. Portman Road;
4. True; 5. The Posh; 6. Sunderland; 7. Austria;
8. Freddie Sears; 9. Walsall; 10. Birmingham.

MY SCORE: /50

★ QUIZ THREE! ★
PAGE 52

WICKED WORDSEARCH!

MY SCORE: /30

PART-TIME PROS!

1. Theo Walcott; 2. Didier Drogba; 3. Glen Johnson; 4. Dimitar Berbatov; 5. Carlos Tevez.

MY SCORE: /20

★ QUIZ FOUR! ★
PAGE 58

BIG TEN – LA LIGA!

1. Karim Benzema; 2. No. 10; 3. Right-back; 4. Espanyol; 5. True; 6. Mattress Makers; 7. Villarreal; 8. Manuel Pellegrini; 9. 25; 10. Deportivo.

MY SCORE: /50

★ QUIZ FIVE! ★
PAGE 64

WICKED WORDSEARCH!

MY SCORE: /30

TITLE WINNERS!

Patrick Vieira and Louis Saha.

MY SCORE: /20

★ QUIZ SIX! ★
PAGE 68

BIG TEN – ENGLAND!

1. France; 2. Man. City; 3. Portugal; 4. Jermain Defoe; 5. Ashley Young; 6. Wayne Rooney; 7. Real Madrid; 8. Two; 9. 25; 10. True.

MY SCORE: /50

★ QUIZ SEVEN! ★
PAGE 74

DREAM TEAM!

GK – Chris Kirkland; RB – Habib Beye; CB – Kolo Toure; CB – Zat Knight; LB – Ashley Cole; CM – Tim Cahill; CM – Rory Delap; LM – Luka Modric; S – Luis Jimenez; S - Darren Bent.

MY SCORE: /30

STADIUM GAME!

1. D; 2. E; 3. C; 4. B; 5. A

MY SCORE: /20

★ QUIZ EIGHT! ★
PAGE 80

BIG TEN – SERIE A!

1. Gianluca Zambrotta; 2. True; 3. Antonio di Natale; 4. Norway; 5. AC Milan; 6. Genoa; 7. Alexandre Pato; 8. Bari; 9. Two; 10. Zlatan Ibrahimovic.

MY SCORE: /50

HOW DID YOU DO?

376-400 PREM CHAMPION!
YOU'VE GOT AN AWESOME FOOTY BRAIN!

351-375 PREM RUNNER-UP!
YOU'RE ALMOST A QUIZ CHAMPION!

301-350 CHAMPO LEAGUE PLACE!
YOU KNOW LOADS OF FOOTY FACTS!

251-300 EUROPA LEAGUE SPOT!
A TOP TRY! WELL DONE!

201-250 MID-TABLE FINISH!
YOU'VE DONE ALRIGHT THIS TIME!

151-200 BOTTOM-HALF FINISH!
YOU NEED TO RAISE YOUR GAME!

0-150 RELEGATION!
THAT'S A REALLY RUBBISH SCORE!

MY TOTAL: /400

MATCH!

THE No.1 FOR FOOTY IN 2010!

BAG YOUR FAVE MAG EVERY TUESDAY!

THE BIGGEST STARS!

THE FA SKILLS!

Improve your game with top tips!

MATCHFACTS!

Mega weekend results round-up!

HOT STUFF!

Check out all the latest footy gear!

ONLINE GAMES!

Play cool games on our website!

FANTASY FOOTY!

Sign up for free and win top prizes!

WICKED MOVIES!

Watch movies at matchmag.co.uk!

LOG ON TO WWW.MATCHMAG.CO.UK

WORLD CUP ACTION!

Can England be crowned world champions for the first time since 1966? The biggest and best World Cup ever kicks off in South Africa in June 2010!

ENGLAND

CHAMPO LEAGUE!

For the first time ever, the final's gonna be on a Saturday! Can Real's new Galacticos win it in Madrid, or will an English club steal the trophy off Barça?

FANTASY FOOTY!

If you missed out on Game One, then log on to matchmag.co.uk and pick your team for Game Two! There are loads of quality prizes to win!

NEW KITS!

Loads of countries are gonna be wearing awesome new shirts for the World Cup! Keep reading MATCH to see England's cool new away kit!

WHAT'S GONNA ROCK IN 2010!

AFRICA CUP OF NATIONS!

Footy superstars Michael Essien, Emmanuel Adebayor and Samuel Eto'o will be battling it out for glory in Angola!

EURO 2012!

England, Scotland, Wales, Northern Ireland and Ireland will find out their qualifying opponents for Euro 2012!

POLAND UKRAINE
candidate for
UEFA EURO 2012

RONALDO v MESSI

The two La Liga heavyweights will lock horns in the Bernabeu in what could be an awesome title decider in April!

MATCH MAGAZINE!

Grab your copy of the UK's best-selling footy mag every week! We have the biggest star interviews and the best free gifts!

THE TRANSFER WINDOW!

We can't wait for loads of clubs to start splashing the cash in the January transfer window! Keep reading MATCH for all the hottest footy gossip!

PREM TITLE RACE!

With Wayne Rooney busting nets and the back four loving clean sheets, Man. United are targeting a fourth title in a row!

HOPE YOU ENJOYED THE 2010 MATCH ANNUAL! SEE YOU NEXT YEAR!